THIS BOOK THINKS YOU'RE A MATH GENIUS

EXPERIMENT IMAGINE CREATE

FILL-IN PAGES FOR YOUR IDEAS

Thames & Hudson

Text by Georgia Amson-Bradshaw
Illustrations by Harriet Russell
Design by Belinda Webster
Math consultancy by Dr Mike Goldsmith

First published in paperback in the United States of America in 2017 by
Thames & Hudson Inc., 500 Fifth Avenue, New York, New York 10110

www.thamesandhudsonusa.com

Library of Congress Control Number 2017931870

ISBN 978-0-500-65117-9

Printed and bound in China by C & C Offset Printed Co. Ltd

Photography credits:
63a - Shutterstock.com, Hein Nouwens

THIS BOOK THINKS YOU'RE A MATH GENIUS

Do you like playing games, creating cool patterns and coloring in? Do you like solving puzzles, baking cakes and sending secret messages? If the answer to these questions is "YES!" it sounds like you might just be... a MATH GENIUS!

Math isn't only about fiendish sums and number-crunching. There's a whole world of mathematical fun to be had right inside this book, so come on math genius, let's go!

CONTENTS

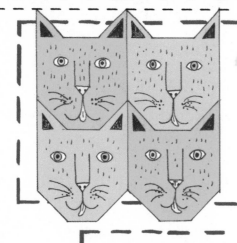

Shapes

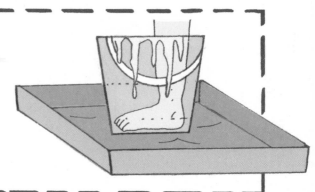

Measurement

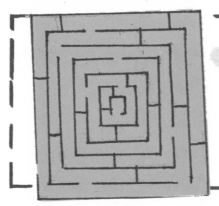

Mazes and Networks

Patterns

Codes and Ciphers

Logic

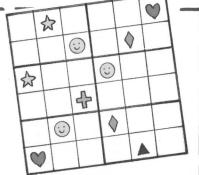

Math Carnival

Math Lab

TILE ANIMAL SHAPES

RAWR! I'm a Tile-ger!

DO THIS!

Create some tessellating animal shapes. Go to page 67 to cut out your tessellation squares to get started.

Make a tessellating shape by cutting pieces out of a square, sliding them to the other side of the square, and sticking them on with tape.

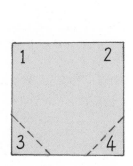 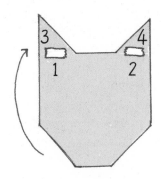

Here's how you make a cat tessellation!

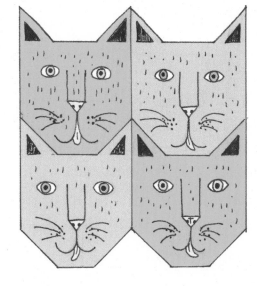

Turn the cat into a bird like this:

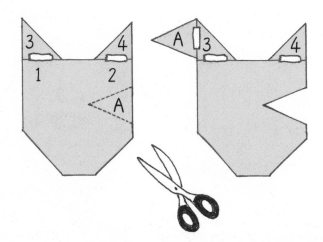

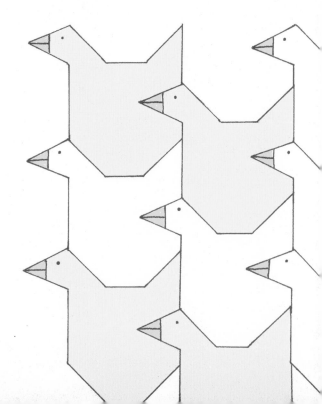

DO THIS!

Try to create some new tessellating animal shapes. What can you come up with? Draw around your paper pieces to see if they tessellate here.

WHERE'S THE MATH?

A tessellation is a geometric pattern of shapes with no overlap and no gaps. A regular tessellation is made up of just one shape. A semi-regular tessellation is made up of two or more shapes.

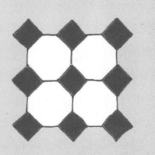

GO ON A TOPOLOGY HUNT

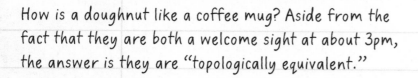

Ah, my favorite sort of math!

How is a doughnut like a coffee mug? Aside from the fact that they are both a welcome sight at about 3pm, the answer is they are "topologically equivalent."

Shapes are topologically equivalent if one can change into another by being stretched, squashed or twisted, but NOT torn.

So a soccer ball is topologically equivalent to a book for example, because it can be reformed into the same shape without tearing.

A soccer ball is NOT topologically equivalent to a doughnut, because a doughnut has a hole in it. The soccer ball would have to be torn to make a doughnut.

DO THIS!

Search your house for objects that are topologically equivalent, and draw them in the chart opposite.

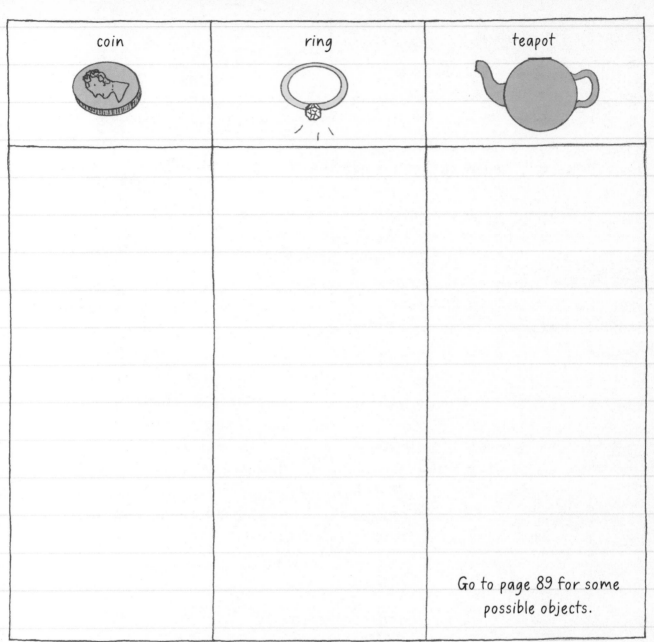

coin	ring	teapot

Go to page 89 for some possible objects.

Absolutely fascinating!

WHERE'S THE MATH?

Topology is a part of geometry, the study of shapes. Topologists study the objects' properties that don't change if the object is stretched, squashed or twisted.

DRAW IN 3D

How do you make a flat drawing look 3D? Simple. You use the POWER OF PROJECTION! But there are different methods for 3D drawing. Try them out here...

DO THIS!

Draw some shapes made of 3D cubes on this squared paper.

I will give you the power to create 3D illusions!

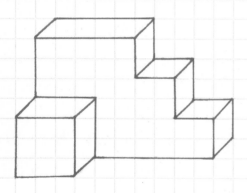

start point

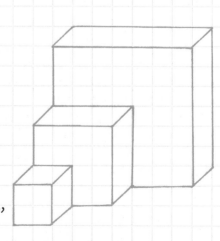

This sort of 3D illusion is called "oblique projection."

Another sort of 3D drawing is called "isometric projection." "Iso" means equal, and "metric" means measure. You can see on this isometric cube that all the central angles are equal, and the lengths of the sides are equal too.

DO THIS!
Draw 3D letters spelling out your initials.

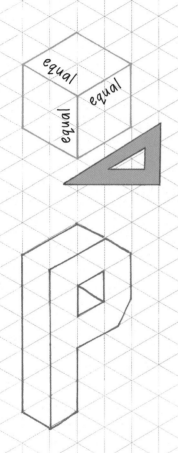

WHERE'S THE MATH?

The two techniques use different angles to create their effects. These projection techniques don't create true perspective drawings because objects are not shown getting smaller into the distance. However, they are useful for making 2D images of 3D objects.

ping!

CHASE MICE ACROSS THE PAGE

DO THIS!

This page has a Mice Problem.
You need to solve it.

Not that sort of problem! The Mice Problem is actually a geometrical problem posed by mathematicians. It goes like this: imagine there are four mice each standing on a corner of a square.

Sorry, we do what now?

Each mouse begins to chase the mouse directly in front, starting at the same moment and moving at the same speed. (Look, just go with it — mathematicians can be really clever but they don't necessarily know about mouse behavior).

What paths do the mice take across the square?

It's possible to draw out the solution by following these steps:

1st
Mark four spots on each side of the square, 1/4 in. from the corners.

2nd
Join the spots up. Then mark four new spots 1/4 in. in on the new, smaller square that has been created.

3rd

Repeat the process over and over again, until you can't draw any smaller squares.

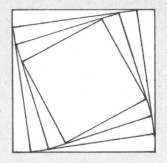

4th

Eventually, four curved lines will appear to spiral in towards the centre from the corners. These trace the paths of the imaginary mice. See a finished one on page 89.

DO THIS!

Finish this one off. Color it in too, if you like.

WHERE'S THE MATH?

These curves are called "pursuit curves" and the math behind them is used in real life to model paths when one moving object is following another, such as a guided missile following a target!

FILL IN A PERSONAL DATA LOG

WARNING: be gentle when measuring your pets, or Tiddles might seek revenge when you are sleeping.

DO THIS!

Log absolutely essential data about yourself, your friends, family and pets in this highly statistical and mathematically complex chart.

	Height in inches	Leg length in inches	Weight of head (to measure, use scales as a pillow)	Distance from being able to lick own elbow in inches
Your name				
Friend's name				
Pet's name				
Name				
Name				
Name				

Think about it... is there any bit of its body your pet doesn't lick...?

You'll need a
measuring tape
for this activity!

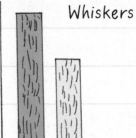

Furthest distance walked while balancing this book on head in feet	Number of whiskers (chin hairs counted on humans)	Distance between eyebrows in inches*	Number of seconds able to not blink	Width of ears in inches

*In some instances eyebrows may need to be applied before measuring...

HAVE A EUREKA MOMENT

Er, excuse me!

DO THIS!

Work out the volume of your foot.

I can't hear anything!

Not that sort of volume!

Volume is a measure of space inside a solid figure, like a cube, a pyramid, or indeed, your foot.

You've probably spent many nights lying awake, wondering exactly what the volume of your foot is. Right? Fortunately, ancient Greek mathematician Archimedes has a solution.

1st

Collect a bowl or bucket, a large tray with edges at least an inch high, and a measuring jug.

2nd
Place the bowl or bucket into the tray, and fill it RIGHT to the top with water. Be careful not to spill any water into the tray.

3rd
Carefully step into the bowl. Water will slosh over the edge into the tray.

4th
Pour the water that sloshed into the tray into the measuring jug. The amount of water that was "displaced" is the exact volume of your foot.

WHERE'S THE MATH?

The story goes that Archimedes realized the volume of an irregular-shaped object could be measured by how much water it "displaces" (pushes out of the way) when he was having a bath. He immediately shouted "eureka!" ("I've got it!") and ran down the street naked. Math makes people do funny things.

BAKE A CAKE WITH MATH

DO THIS!

Become a baking genius... using math!

Oh hello dearie!

Want to know how granny won the village cake-baking contest for ten years in a row?

The secret is... Granny is a stone-cold math genius. Cakes, cookies, batters... they all use flour, fat (butter or oil), egg and sugar. To make them into delicious food, mix 'em up using ratios!

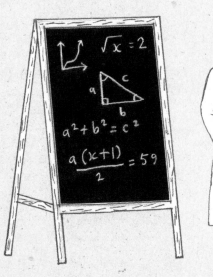

On the chalkboard:

$$\sqrt{x} = 2$$

$$a^2 + b^2 = c^2$$

$$\frac{a(x+1)}{2} = 59$$

Here's a pie chart showing the parts for shortbread cookies:

Mix the butter and sugar together, add the flour and mix into a dough. Roll it out, cut it into cookie shapes and bake at 390°F until golden.

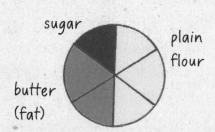

sugar

plain flour

butter (fat)

1 part sugar
2 parts butter
3 parts flour

What's a "part?"

The beauty of ratios is you can make one "part" however big you need, and the basic recipe stays the same. So for shortbread, if one part is 2 oz, you'd need 6 oz of flour, 4 oz of butter and 2 oz of sugar.

DO THIS!

Figure out the amounts you need for a sponge cake, and bake it!

Here's a pie chart showing the weight ratios for a sponge cake. To get the amount for one "part," start with the eggs. Two eggs make enough mixture for one regular cake, so first weigh two eggs.

Next, write in the weight you need for each ingredient on the dotted lines in the pie chart.

Cream the butter and sugar together until pale and fluffy, then mix in the eggs and the flour.

Pour the mixture into a greased cake tin, and bake for about half an hour at 390°F.

sugar	self-raising flour
butter	eggs

This cake is one part math, one part deliciousness!

WHERE'S THE MATH?

Ratios are how we can show the relative difference between amounts. They are a quick and easy way to scale up amounts, like in recipes.

ESCAPE ANY MAZE

Have you heard of a labyrinth? It's a sort of maze, except you can't get lost. You just follow a single path and eventually you get to the center. A simple labyrinth looks like this:

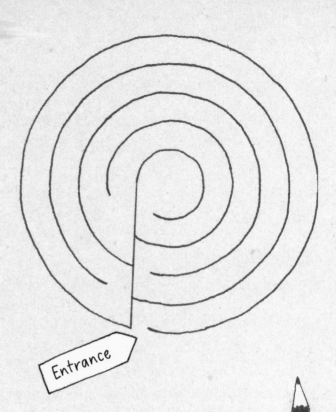

Entrance

Pretty pointless maze if you can't get lost!

DO THIS!

Draw a copy of the labyrinth above. BUT here's the twist: figure out a way to draw it in less than 30 seconds, without copying from the original. Here's a clue: use a pencil with an eraser. Solution on page 90.

DO THIS!

Find the correct path through the maze. There's a simple way to do this: look for dead ends, and block them out by coloring them in. You'll create more dead ends as you color. Eventually the path will be revealed…

This dead end has been colored in

Who says coloring in isn't math?

WHERE'S THE MATH?

Remember topology from pages 8-9? A maze is a topological puzzle. By coloring in the dead ends, you keep the basic topological shape of the maze the same, but it becomes simple enough to see the route through.

PLOT A PATH WITHOUT LIFTING YOUR PEN

Meet Leonhard Euler (sounds like "oiler"), a mathematician from the 18th century, who had a problem. He liked to go for walks* but he didn't like to retrace his steps at any point. That would be a boring walk.

> Dear diary, today I went on a really boring walk...

This is a map of Königsberg, where Euler wanted to go for a walk. There are seven bridges. Euler wanted to know if it was possible to take a walk that visits each part of the town, but crosses each bridge only once.

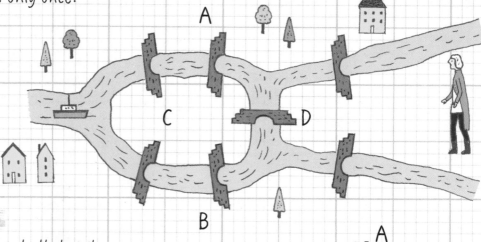

DO THIS!

Try to figure out a route that visits every piece of land, but crosses each bridge only once. Can it be done?

You can label the parts of the town A-D to help you keep track...

...and even turn the map into a "graph" like this.

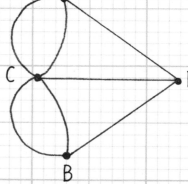

*Maybe. This fact is not actually recorded in the history books.

DO THIS!

Have a go at these puzzles too! Which ones can you plot a path on that visits every dot without lifting your pen, but never traces the same line twice?

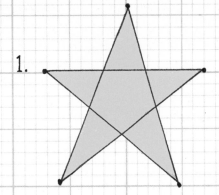

1.

2.

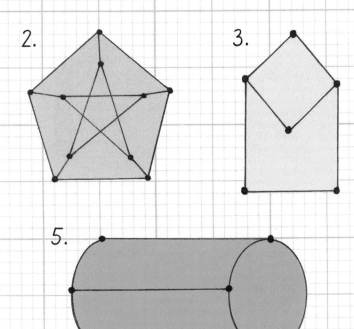

3.

4.

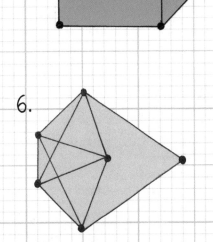

5.

6.

Can you figure out what links the graphs that cross every dot but only go along each line once? Answer on page 91.

I'm a STAR!!

Actually, you're a graph

WHERE'S THE MATH?

This sort of math is called "graph theory," and it was first developed by Euler. The diagrams are called graphs too — but they are different to graphs such as bar graphs that show statistics.

PLAY MATHEMATICAL GUESS WHO

Are you ready for some detective work?

DO THIS!

Work out who is who in this graph, using these clues.

1. Alice has four friends: Becky, Chloe, Dana and Emma.
2. Emma is Freya's only friend.
3. Becky and Emma are Chloe's friends.

Write the letters A–F next to the faces to stand for the girls' names.

I've cracked some tough cases... but none as hard as "who is Freya?"

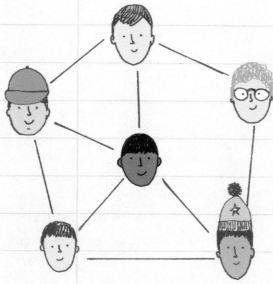

DO THIS!

Identify which boy is which.

1. Cyril has two friends, Deepak and Amit.
2. Bryn is friends with Eli, Deepak and Faisal.
3. Eli has more friends than Faisal.

Answers on page 91.

DO THIS!

On this page, draw your own graph showing who is friends with who in your class.

WHERE'S THE MATH?

In these puzzles, graphs are used to model a network of friends. Mathematicians use graph theory to show relationships between different things, for example it can show the relationships between animal species in biology.

Whaddup, cuz?

CREATE A PATTERN WITH NUMBERS

DO THIS!

1st Think of a few random numbers. Let's use Leonardo da Vinci's birthday: 15th day of the 4th month, 1452. We'll break that up into 1, 5, 4, 1, 4, 5, 2.

Happy birthday to me!

2nd Pick a start point, and use your numbers to tell you the line length to draw in squares. Spin the page a right angle (90 degrees) clockwise after you've drawn each line, like this:

6th   2nd

7th   3rd   5th   1st   start point

4th

3rd After the final number, simply start the sequence again. Some sequences come round in a loop, while others just keep heading off in one direction.

start point

Color the sections in if you like!

Try your own patterns on this page.

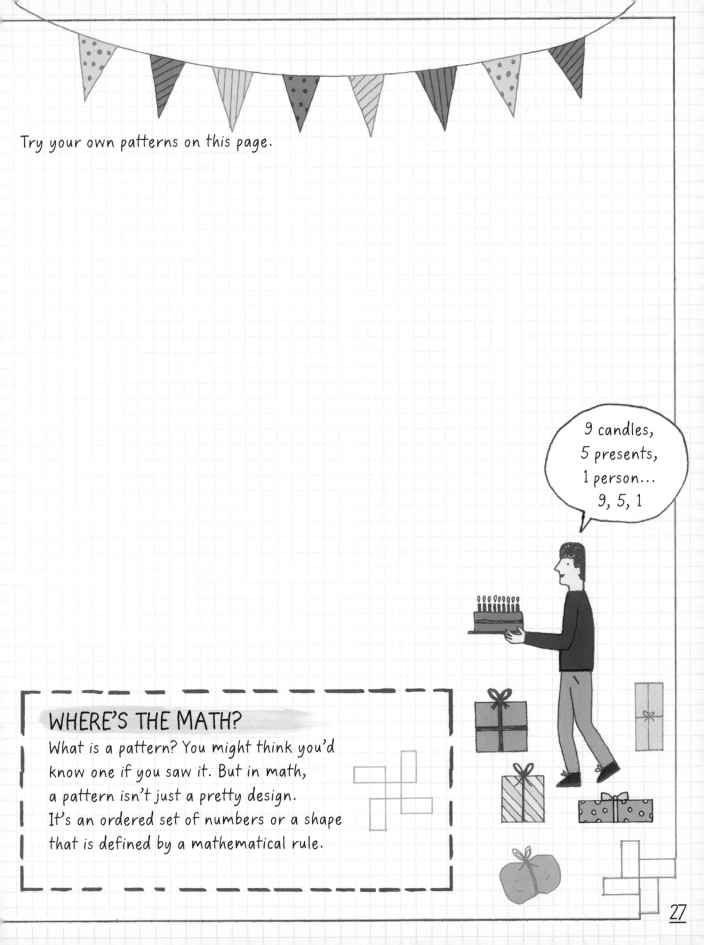

9 candles,
5 presents,
1 person...
9, 5, 1

WHERE'S THE MATH?

What is a pattern? You might think you'd
know one if you saw it. But in math,
a pattern isn't just a pretty design.
It's an ordered set of numbers or a shape
that is defined by a mathematical rule.

FIND THE HIDDEN RULE

This way

LEFT RIGHT

DO THIS!

Look at the six shapes on the left. These shapes ALL follow the same single rule. Now look at the shapes on the right. Those six shapes do NOT follow the rule. What is the rule?

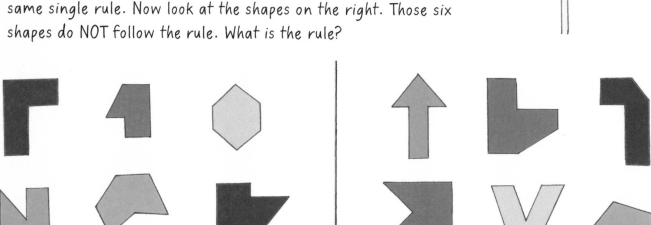

Answer: all the shapes on the left have six sides.
The shapes on the right do not have six sides.
Easy now you know!

DO THIS!

Try these puzzles too. Remember, left-hand pictures
follow the rule, right-hand pictures don't. Answers on page 92.

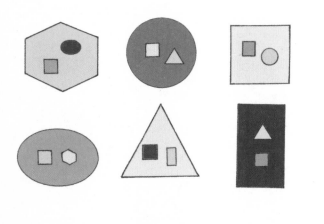
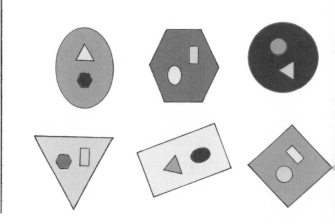

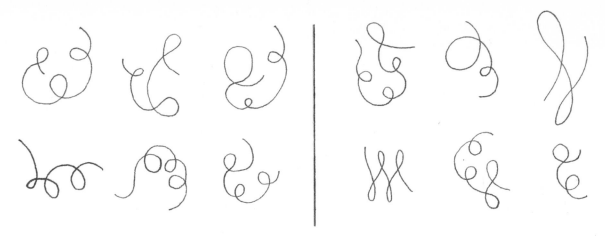

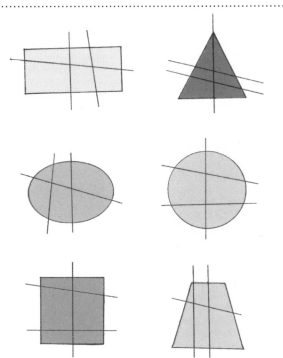

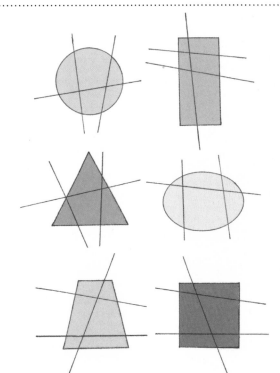

WHERE'S THE MATH?

On the previous page you made patterns by following a mathematical rule — making quarter turns between drawing each number in a sequence. This is the opposite. You can see the patterns that have been drawn — but what rules do they follow?

He doesn't follow the rules!

GROW A FRACTAL TREE, BLOW FRACTAL BUBBLES

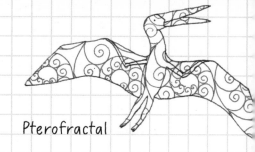

Pterofractal

DO THIS!

Draw a vertical line for a trunk. Ours is 8 squares tall. At the top of the line, draw two lines, or branches, forking off at a diagonal. They should diagonally cross half as many squares as the trunk (4 squares).

At the end of each branch, add two more lines forking off at a diagonal, crossing the same number of squares as the first two branches (4 squares). At the end of those, add two branches half as long (2 squares), then another set 2 squares long branching off those. Keep going until you can't go any smaller!

Diagonal

4 squares

4 squares

2 squares

8 squares

The lengths of the trunk and branches get shorter like this: 8, 4, 4, 2, 2, 1, 1, 0.5, 0.5, and so on... forever!

Draw over and complete this tree. Start here.

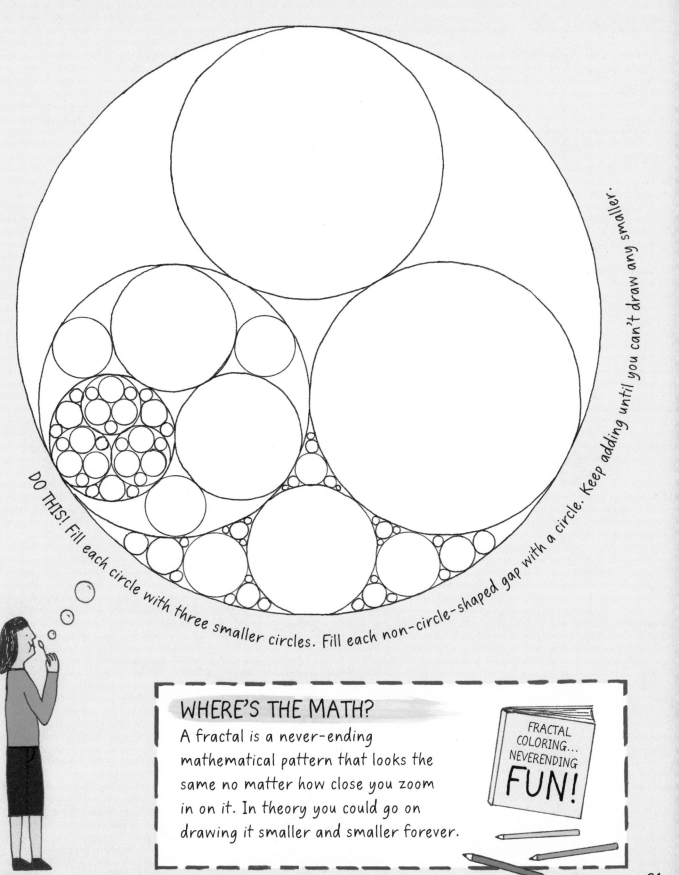

DO THIS! Fill each circle with three smaller circles. Fill each non-circle-shaped gap with a circle. Keep adding until you can't draw any smaller.

WHERE'S THE MATH?

A fractal is a never-ending mathematical pattern that looks the same no matter how close you zoom in on it. In theory you could go on drawing it smaller and smaller forever.

FRACTAL COLORING... NEVERENDING FUN!

SPOT PASCAL'S PATTERNS

DO THIS!

Color in any number patterns that you find on the triangles. The bees have some ideas...

Color even and odd numbers different colors.

1

1 1

1 2 1

1 3 3 1

1 4 6 4 1

1 5 10 10 5 1

1 6 15 20 15 6 1

1 7 21 35 35 21 7 1

1 8 28 56 70 56 28 8 1

1 9 36 84 126 126 84 36 9 1

1 10 45 120 210 252 210 120 45 10 1

1 11 55 165 330 462 462 330 165 55 11 1

1 12 66 220 495 792 924 792 495 220 66 12 1

1 13 78 286 715 1287 1716 1716 1287 715 286 78 13 1

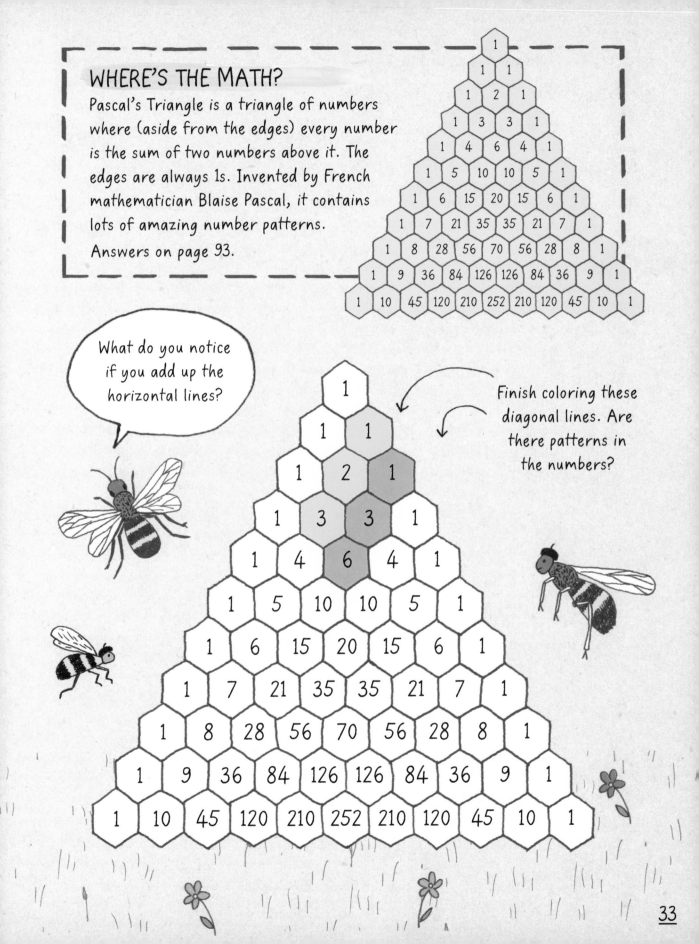

WHERE'S THE MATH?

Pascal's Triangle is a triangle of numbers where (aside from the edges) every number is the sum of two numbers above it. The edges are always 1s. Invented by French mathematician Blaise Pascal, it contains lots of amazing number patterns.

Answers on page 93.

What do you notice if you add up the horizontal lines?

Finish coloring these diagonal lines. Are there patterns in the numbers?

SEND A SECRET MESSAGE

The name's Caesar...
Julius Caesar.

DO THIS!

Look at this encrypted message. Can you read it?

> ## FDHVDU LV D MHUN

Stuck? Here's a clue... move back three.

A B C D E F G H I J K L M N O P Q R S T U V W X Y Z

Got it yet? The secret message above is written using the Caesar Cipher. When Julius Caesar was out conquering, he needed to send secret messages to his generals.

He used a cipher. He would replace the letters in his message with the letter 3 places along in the alphabet. So A becomes D, B becomes E, etc. At the end of the alphabet you just shift round to the beginning again.

Write out your own secret message using the Caesar Cipher here.

The ancient Greek Spartans used "scytales" to send secret messages.

To make a scytale, each person needs a standard-sized pencil, a paper strip and some tape.

DO THIS!
Go to page 69 and cut out the scytale strips.

1st

Tape your strip at one end of your pencil.
Wrap the scytale strip around the pencil so the edges meet but don't overlap.

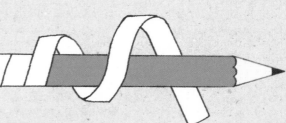

2nd

Tape the other end in place, and write your message along the pencil.

MEET AT 12 NOON

3rd

Unwrap the strip, and send it to your friend.
In order to read the message they must wrap the strip around a pencil exactly the same size as yours.

Red squirrel has dropped his nuts...

WHERE'S THE MATH?

Codes and ciphers are not exactly the same thing. A code substitutes each word for another word (like using a foreign-language dictionary). A cipher mixes up the existing letters in a message according to a rule (like "move along three").

BREAK THE ENCRYPTED PICTURE

It's all Greek to me... so I understand it perfectly!

DO THIS!

Look at this Polybius square. It's an ancient Greek invention for writing coded messages. Using this type of encryption, numbers are used to give co-ordinates for letters. You look at the horizontal number first, and the vertical one second. So "HELLO" becomes 32, 51, 23, 23, 53.

	1	2	3	4	5
1	A	B	C	D	E
2	F	G	H	I	J
3	K	L	M	N	O
4	P	Q	R	S	T
5	U	V	W	X	YZ

But a Polybius square could encrypt something other than letters. It could be colors instead.

Here's a simple flower with the codes for its colors shown.

	1	2	3	4
1				
2				
3				
4				

14	34	14
34	33	34
14	34	14
22	22	14
14	22	14

You could write out the code for the flower like this:
14, 34, 14 / 34, 33, 34 / 14, 34, 14 / 22, 22, 14 / 14, 22, 14.

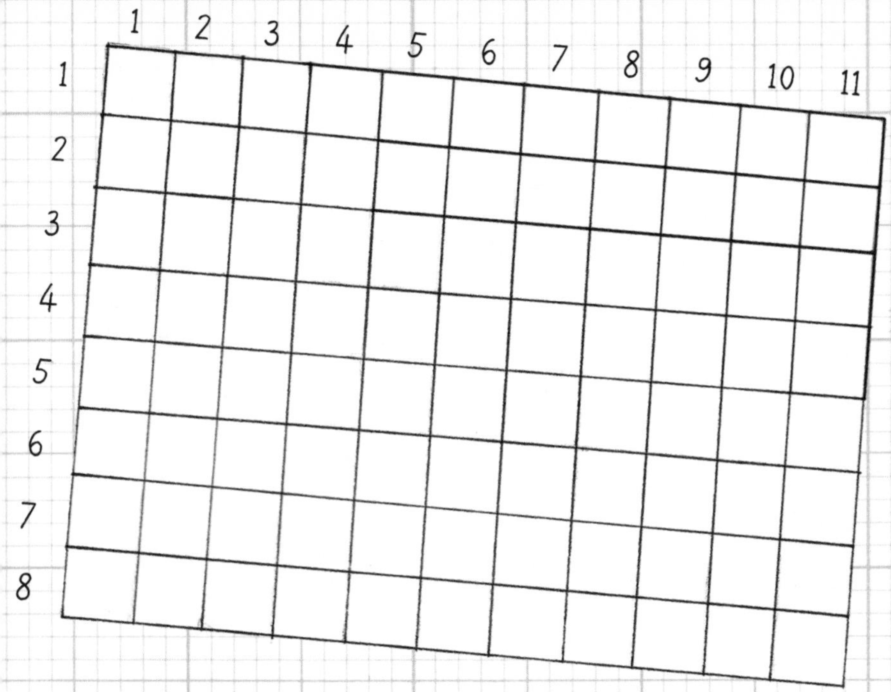

The grid across the top is labeled with columns 1–11 and rows 1–8.

DO THIS!

Color a picture of your own in this grid, then write out the code for it on another piece of paper. Send the code to a friend along with the Polybius square, and challenge them to redraw your image.

DO THIS!

Find the picture hidden in the grid below
Solution on page 94.

32	32	13	13	13	13	13	13	13	13	13	13	13	13	32	32
32	32	13	23	23	23	23	23	23	23	23	23	23	13	32	32
32	32	32	13	42	42	42	42	42	42	42	42	13	32	32	32
32	32	13	42	42	42	42	42	42	42	42	42	13	32	32	32
32	13	42	42	42	42	42	42	42	42	42	42	42	13	32	
13	14	42	42	42	21	21	21	21	21	42	42	42	42	23	13
13	23	42	42	21	12	41	12	12	41	21	42	42	42	23	13
13	14	42	21	41	12	12	41	41	12	12	21	42	21	23	13
13	23	21	12	41	44	12	12	12	12	12	12	21	21	23	13
13	23	21	12	12	41	12	12	41	41	41	41	21	21	23	13
13	23	42	21	41	41	41	12	12	41	12	21	42	21	23	13
13	23	42	42	21	12	12	12	41	12	21	42	42	42	23	13
32	23	42	22	42	21	21	21	21	21	42	42	22	42	23	13
32	13	42	22	42	42	42	42	42	42	42	42	22	42	13	32
32	32	13	22	22	23	23	23	23	23	23	22	22	13	32	32
32	32	32	13	22	13	13	13	13	13	13	22	13	32	32	32

WHERE'S THE MATH?

The Polybius square gives you the co-ordinates for your colors. Co-ordinates are a set of numbers that show an exact position. They are used on graphs and maps.

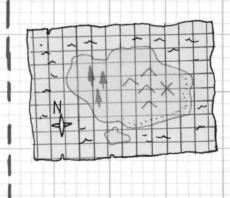

READ LIKE A COMPUTER

DO THIS!

Numbers can be broken down into their 1s, 10s, 100s, and so on, like this:

This is because we use the decimal system, or base 10. It's all multiples of 10!

4,325 can be broken down into:

1000s	100s	10s	1s
4	3	2	5

The binary system is the type of counting that computers use. It means counting in base 2. In base 2, instead of the columns getting 10 times bigger each time, they get two times bigger.

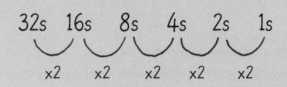

So in order to write the number 1 in binary, you put a 1 in the first (1s) column. But to write the number two, you put a 1 in the 2s column, and 0 in the 1s. So it looks like this: 10.

32s	16s	8s	4s	2s	1s
				1	0

To make number 7, you need to add up to 7 using these multiples of 2. You'd need to add 1, 2, and 4 together. So put 1 in the 4s, 1 in the 2s, and 1 in the 1s, so 7 is written as 111.

32s	16s	8s	4s	2s	1s
			1	1	1

To make number 18 you'd need 1 in the 16s column, 0 in the 8s, 0 in the 4s, 1 in the 2s, and 0 in the 1s. Like this: 10010.

32s	16s	8s	4s	2s	1s
	1	0	0	1	0

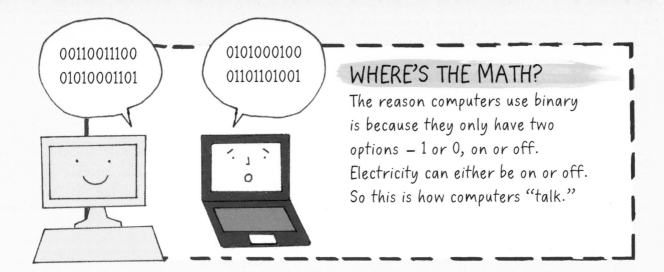

WHERE'S THE MATH?

The reason computers use binary is because they only have two options — 1 or 0, on or off. Electricity can either be on or off. So this is how computers "talk."

DO THIS!

Now you know how to write binary, color in this picture by writing the numbers at the side. Color a square black for a 1, and leave it white for a 0. The grid is split in half so you never have to write a number higher than 31.

The first three numbers have been done for you.

Zero = 00000=
Six = 00110=
Twelve = 01100=

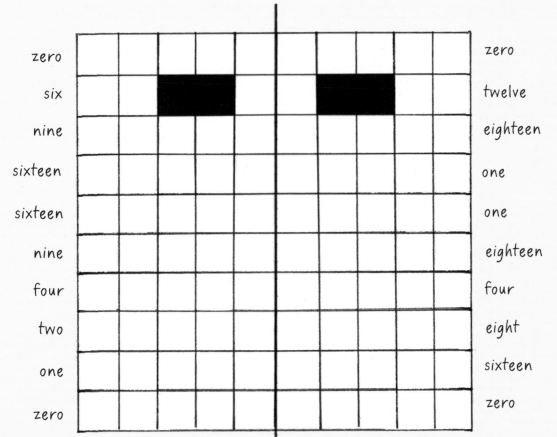

What picture is revealed? Answer on page 94.

COMPLETE THE GRIDS

DO THIS!

Solve this sudoku puzzle. The rules are: each of the four boxes has to contain all the numbers 1 to 4. Each number can only appear once in a row, column or box.

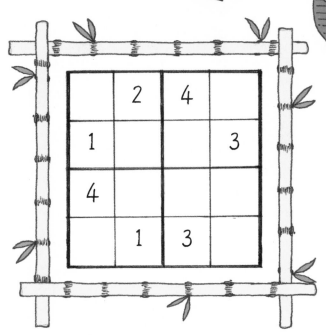

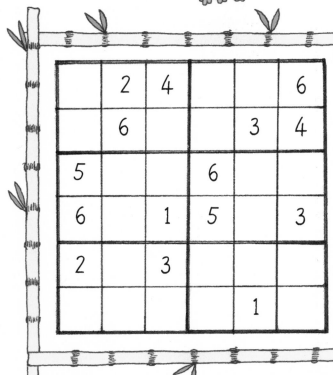

DO THIS!

Now try this one. Each box must contain all the numbers 1 to 6. Each number can only appear once in a row, column or box.

One, two, three…
Ichi, ni, san…

DO THIS!
Now you've got the hang of it, try this full-size puzzle with nine boxes. Make sure each row, column and box features the numbers 1 to 9 only once. Solutions are all on page 95!

WHERE'S THE MATH?
These sorts of logic puzzles are very popular in Japan (and elsewhere!). Although sudoku puzzles use numbers, the numbers could be replaced by any set of symbols.

DETECT TRUTH AND LIES

DO THIS!

Figure out how many liars there are.

In Nightmare Castle honorable knights ALWAYS tell the truth, and dishonorable knaves ALWAYS lie. Unfortunately, they look exactly the same.

Derek is a pigeon-liver'd knave!

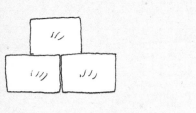

The puzzle...
You meet two guards, Derek and Jason. They both say the other is a lying knave. How many people are truthful knights, none, one or two?

Hint! A good way to try and solve it is to go through the options in your head, or by writing it down. So if Jason is telling the truth, does that make Derek a knight or a knave, and vice versa. You can then figure out how many knights there are and how many knaves, even without knowing who is which.

WHERE'S THE MATH?

Logical reasoning is a way of thinking things through systematically in order to solve problems. In school, this sort of thinking is normally applied to problems involving numbers or letters, but it can be used in many situations. The answer to this logic puzzle is on page 95.

BE A NIM NINJA

DO THIS FIRST!
Cut out your nim pieces and learn to play on page 59.

Grand Master, please teach me the ways of nim.

To be a nim ninja, you must understand the secret of the nim sum. Let us begin.

First you must think like a computer and convert numbers into binary. Learn about this on page 38. Off you go Grasshopper!

In this example the rows contain 4, 5 and 3 pieces. In binary those are written: 100, 101 and 11.

4   1 0 0

5   1 0 1

3   1 1

Next, add up the columns of the binary numbers, and see if you get an odd or even number. Here we get 2, 1, 2, so even, odd, even.

Now, rewrite the even numbers as 0s, and the odd number as 1s. This makes the <u>nim sum</u>. Here it is 010.

So let's imagine you're playing and it's your turn first.

```
1 0 0
1 0 1
  1 1
───────
2 1 2
↓ ↓ ↓
even, odd, even
↓
0 1 0
```

nim sum

On your turn, you know from the nim sum if you're winning or losing. With all 0s, you're losing. If you have any 1s, you're winning.

0 1 0

I'm winning!

0 1 0

WHERE'S THE MATH?

Nim sums aren't just used in this game. Computers use binary, and nim sums form the basis of many computer processes.

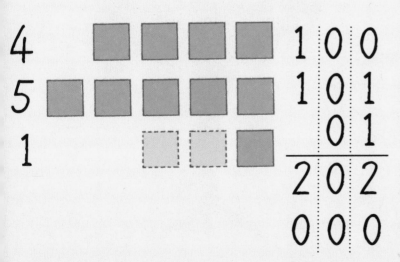

```
4   1 0 0
5   1 0 1
      0 1
1   ─────
    2 0 2
    0 0 0
```

To win, take away pieces so that the nim sum at the start of the next person's turn becomes all 0s. In our game, taking two pieces off the bottom row gives us all even numbers, or a nim sum of 000.

Each turn, take away pieces so that the nim sum after your go is 0s, and eventually you will win.

CHANCE YOUR LUCK IN A GAME OF PIG

Are you a greedy pig, or will you bring home the bacon in this game of probability?

DO THIS!

Grab one or more friends to play with, and a pencil and paper to record scores.

1st

Take turns rolling two dice. Roll the two dice as many times as you like on your turn, adding the up score in your head after each roll. The aim is to get to 100 first.

2nd

When you decide to stop rolling, add the score from that turn to your total from your previous rounds. BUT...

Two sixes, bad luck!

3rd

Be careful! If you roll a six on one of the dice, you score zero for that round and your turn ends. If you roll two sixes, your entire score so far goes back to zero. So don't be a greedy pig!

DO THIS!

Go to page 85 and make two dice for playing Pig.

Cross my trotters it's not two sixes

WHERE'S THE MATH?

Pig is a game of probability. Probability is how likely something is to happen, and we can describe it using fractions. For example, if you roll a single six-sided die, there are six possible outcomes, so there is a 1/6 chance of rolling a 6. If you have two six-sided dice, there are 36 possible outcomes, so you have a 1/36 chance of rolling double sixes.

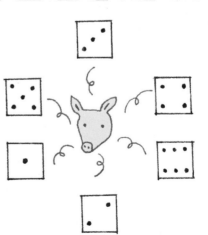

READ MINDS WITH MATH

Welcome to Madam Esmerelda's
Math-magical
Mind-Reading Tent...

DO THIS!

1. Think of a three-digit number with decreasing digits (such as 852).

2. Reverse the order of the digits (258).

3: Subtract the number in step 2 from the number in step 1 (852 - 258 = 594)

4. Reverse the order of the answer you get in step 3 (495).

5. Add the numbers from step 3 and step 4 (594 + 495).

Your answer is... 1,089! Try this on a friend. Have them do the steps without showing you their numbers. Amaze them when you can "read their mind" by revealing their answer is 1,089.

DO THIS!

Go to page 87 and cut out the Math Mind-Reading cards.

1st

Have your friend pick a number from 1 to 31 but keep their number secret.

2nd

Ask them to point to the cards that have their number on, still keeping their number secret. For example, if they choose 19, they will point to cards 4, 1, and 0.

3rd

Add up the first number listed on those cards (in this case 16, 2 and 1). This gives their number. Blow their mind when you reveal you know it!

WHERE'S THE MATH?

What do you notice about the first numbers listed on each card, 16, 8, 4, 2 and 1? Answer: they are powers of two, or the place values in binary! Pointing to the cards with their number on tells you in binary what their chosen number is.

I'm hearing a number... it could be a one... or a zero...

PLAY QUICK-DRAW ARITHMETIC

16... 20... 4

Here's a game for a coupl'a gun-slingin' rodeo-ridin' math-maniacs. You need at least two players, and someone else to be the caller.

DO THIS!

1st

Two duelers (players) stand back-to-back. The caller shouts out a number as the starting number, such as "32."

2nd

The caller then shouts out operations, such as "minus 16... plus 4... divided by 5." Each time the caller shouts an operation, the duelers take a step away from one another.

3rd

The duelers must keep a running total of the sum in their heads, for example 32 minus 16 plus 4 divided by 5 is 4. After the caller has shouted out a few operations, they can call "DRAW!"

4th

When the caller shouts "DRAW!" the duellers spin around and shout out what they think the correct total is. The winner is the quickest to shout the correct answer.

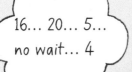

If both duelers get it right at the same time, they go again. If one gets it wrong or is slower, that player is out, and another swaps in to take on the surviving player.

Tip
It's easier for the caller to have the sums written down and worked out beforehand. That way they aren't trying to keep up with the players in their own head!

16... 20... 5... no wait... 4

32 minus 16... plus 4... divided by 5...

WHERE'S THE MATH?
This game is based on simple arithmetic - adding, subtracting, multiplying and dividing. It's all about getting super speedy at mental math. Are you the fastest number-slinger in the West?

WANTED
100
MATHEMATICIAN

THIS BOOK THINKS IT'S A MATH LAB

This section of the book contains pages for you to cut out, cut up, fold and stick.

CUT COOL KIRIGAMI PATTERNS

Kirigami is the Japanese technique of paper folding and cutting. Follow these instructions to make some amazing mathematical, symmetrical paper art.

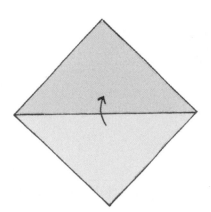

DO THIS!

1st

Cut out the square template, kirigami piece 1, on page 55. Fold it in half from point to point to make a triangle shape, with the design on the outside.

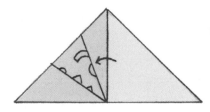

2nd

Fold the new triangle in half again to make a smaller triangle, again keeping the design on the outside.

3rd

Rotate your triangle so the point faces down. Flip it over so the design is underneath. Fold the right side in, then the left side in so they are of equal size. The left side has the design on.

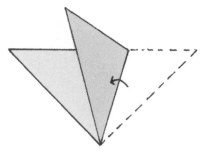

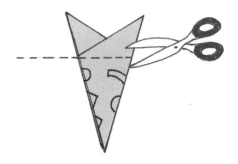

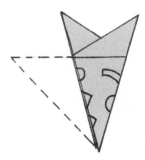

4th

Snip off the top points. Turn the triangle over then cut around the design. Unfold to reveal your cool kirigami pattern!

DO THIS!

Make a five-pointed kirigami flower.

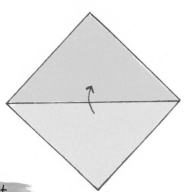

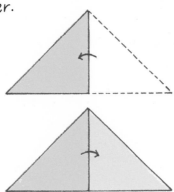

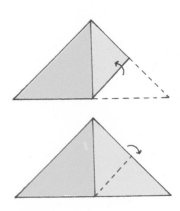

1st

Cut out the square template on page 57: kirigami piece 2. Fold it in half into a triangle shape.

2nd

Fold it in half again, then unfold, making a crease down the center line of your triangle.

3rd

Take the right-hand point and fold it upwards to meet the top point. Unfold it again, leaving a crease halfway along the right-hand edge of the triangle.

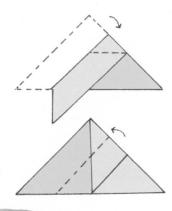

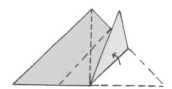

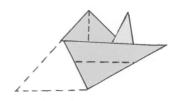

4th

Fold the left-hand edge over in a straight line to meet the middle of the right-hand edge. Unfold, leaving the crease.

5th

Fold the right-hand point upwards so its edge lines up with the new crease you just made.

6th

Fold the whole left-hand point over so the bottom edge lines up with the right-hand edge.

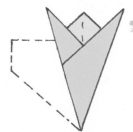

7th

Keeping the point at the bottom, fold the right-hand edge over to meet the left-hand edge.

8th

Draw one half of a petal shape, and cut it out. Unfold to reveal your flower!

The design. When folded,
cut away the white parts.

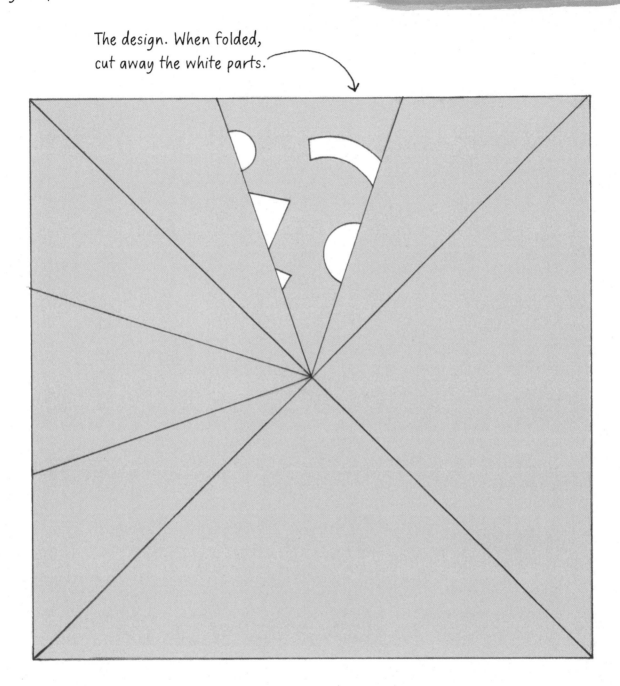

This is a six-pointed design. Did you know
snowflakes naturally have six sides?

A petal design template to draw onto your kirigami flower, to cut out and unfold.

LEARN TO PLAY NIM

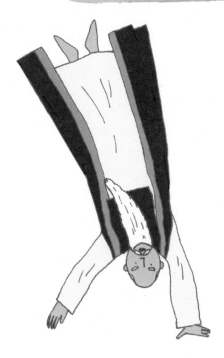

> Greetings, Grasshopper. Before you can become a nim ninja, you must first learn the ancient rules of nim.

DO THIS!

Cut out the nim pieces on the next page.

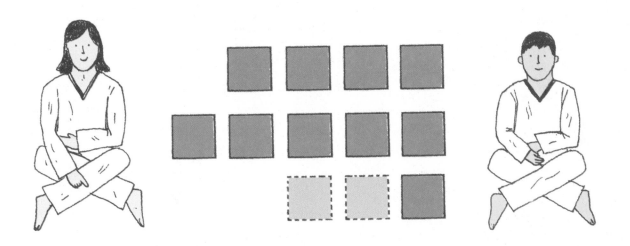

Arrange any number of pieces into any number of rows. You don't have to use all of the pieces in every game. Here we've chosen to create three rows, containing four, five and three pieces.

Take it in turns to remove pieces. Players can remove any number of pieces, as long as they all come from the same row. They must remove at least one piece per turn. Here, player one has removed two pieces from the second row.

Here, player two has taken all three pieces from the third row on their turn.

The person who takes the last piece (or pieces) away is the winner.

DO THIS!

Cut along the dotted lines to make
your square nim pieces

TOWERS OF HANOI

Legend goes that a secret order of monks, somewhere in Vietnam, are tasked with moving 64 golden rings one at a time between three pegs. When they finally finish moving all 64 rings, the world will end. Eek! But do you need to be worried? Try the puzzle out for yourself!

DO THIS!

1st

Cut out the discs and numbered tabs on the next page. These are your game pieces.

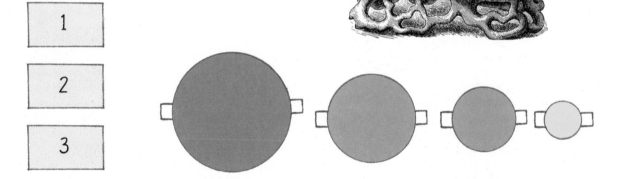

2nd

On a table or flat surface, place the numbered tabs so they create three "columns." Stack the discs next to the first tab, biggest disc at the bottom, smallest at the top.

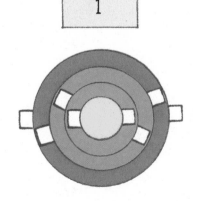

The aim is to move all the discs from column 1 to column 3 in as few moves as possible.

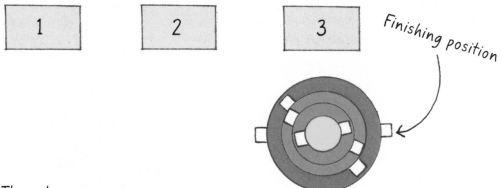

Finishing position

However! The rules are:

1. You can only move one disc at a time.

2. You cannot put a larger disc on top of a smaller disc.

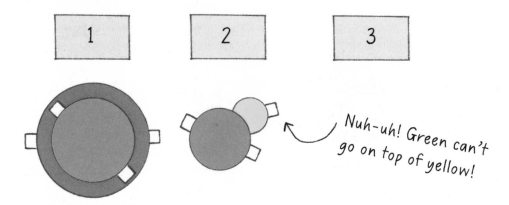

Nuh-uh! Green can't go on top of yellow!

Can you figure out the quickest way to get all four discs from column 1 to column 3? You should be able to do it in fifteen moves.

Solution on page 95!

WHERE'S THE MATH?

An algorithm is a set of rules or instructions that must be completed in the right order to solve a problem. The step-by-step solution to this puzzle is a type of algorithm.

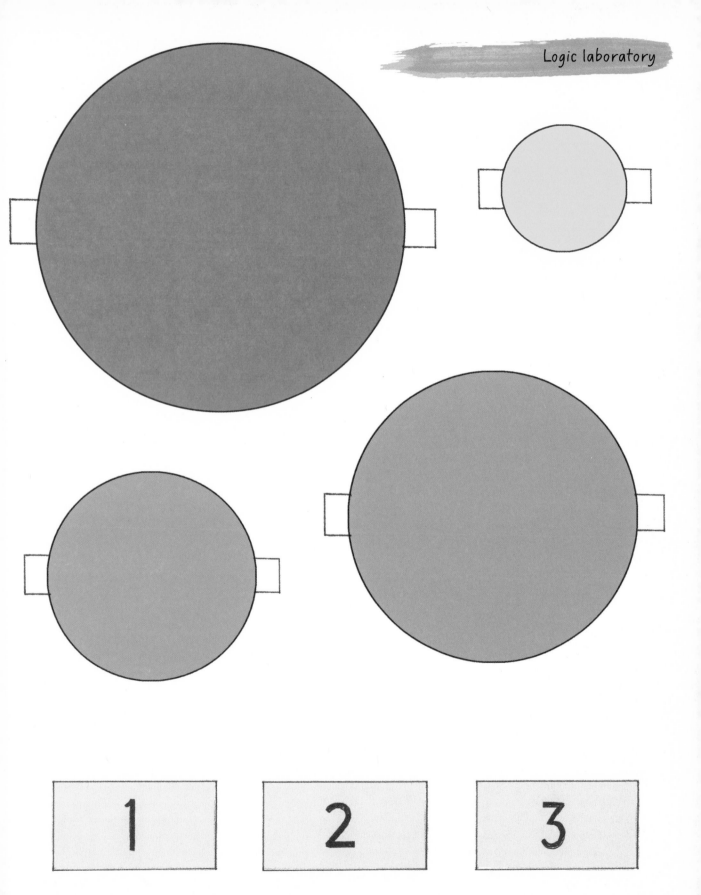

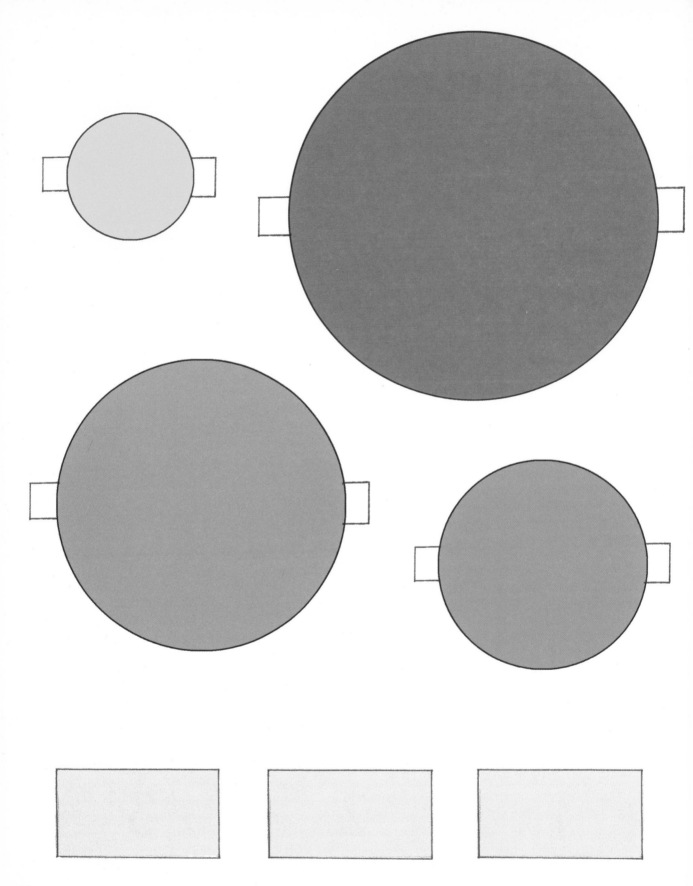

TESSELLATION SQUARES

DO THIS!

Cut these squares out and use them for
the tessellation animal challenge on page 6.

SCYTALES STRIPS

DO THIS!

1st

Cut out these strips.

2nd

Find a regular pencil, of standard size.

3rd

Wrap the strips around the pencil. Can you get them to line up correctly, so you can see the hidden pictures?

4th

Use the blank ones to write on, and create your own secret messages! Instructions are on page 35.

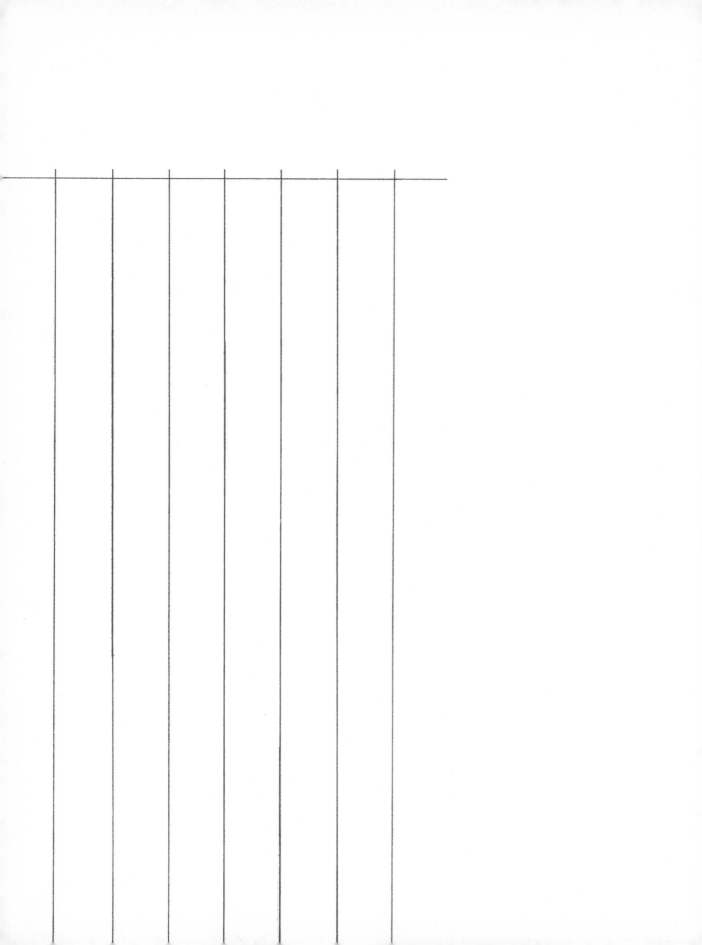

3D PERSPECTIVE ILLUSION

Perspective drawing is a way of creating the illusion of depth. In real life, objects in the distance look smaller, so we can use perspective to trick our brains into misjudging the size of objects.

So which tree is bigger? The one at the back, right? Wrong! They are both the same size.

DO THIS!

Test this illusion for yourself with the trees below and the landscape on the next page. Cut along the dotted line below, then cut the two trees out. On the next page, try placing them at different intervals along the road. See how the one at the front always appears smaller than the one at the back.

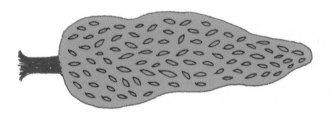

HEXAFLEXAGON

Make a crazy flexing hexagon with hidden sides. You just need scissors and glue.

DO THIS!

Cut out the templates on the next page. Let's start with the colored one.

1st

Fold the template lengthways down the middle line to make it double thickness. Glue it shut, so you have a long, flat strip. Let the glue dry completely.

2nd

Using a ruler and an empty ballpoint pen or a butter knife, score along all the fold lines, and fold them backwards and forwards a few times so they are very flexible.

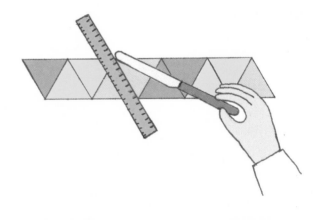

3rd

Lay your scored strip out in front of you like this, with the glue tabs facing down, and the green triangle to your left.

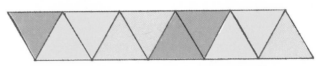

4th

Fold back the strip at the fold between the third triangle (yellow), and the fourth triangle (blue). It should look like this:

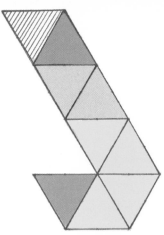

5th

Fold the strip backwards again between the fifth (yellow) triangle, and the sixth triangle (blue). You should have this shape:

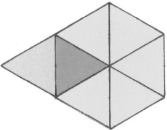

6th

Tuck the green triangle behind the yellow triangle beneath it. Flip it over, and fold the final triangle down so the two glue tabs are touching face-to-face. Glue them together. Wait for the glue to dry.

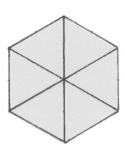

7th

To flex your hexaflexagon, pinch three alternate corners together. You can then open up a new face from the center of the hexaflexagon.

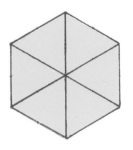

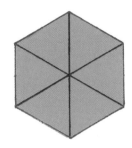

TA-DA! Your flexagon is complete. You can now color in your blank template to create a flexagon design of your own. What will you draw on yours?

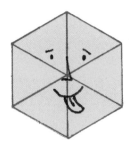

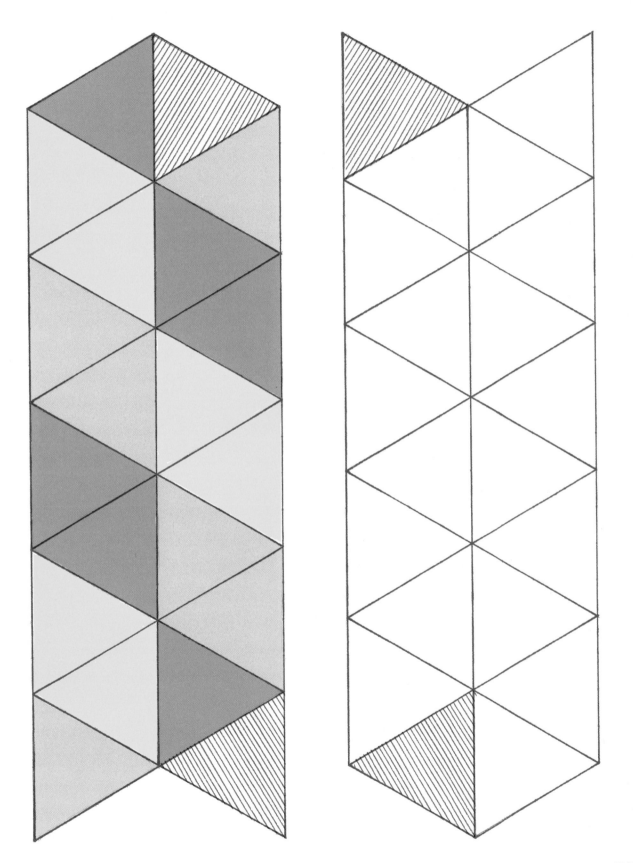

MIND-BENDING MÖBIUS STRIPS

> My strips will really send you round the twist!

DO THIS!

Cut out each of the strips on the next page. Get some glue or tape, and prepare to see some amazing möbius magic!

1st

Take strip number one. Make a half twist in it and tape or glue the ends together.

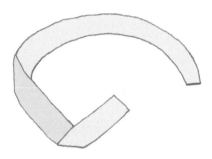

2nd

Cut along the line of 1s that runs all the way through the middle. What happens?

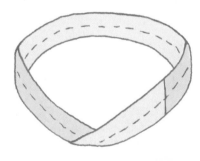

3rd

Take strip number two. Make a full twist in it and tape or glue the ends together.

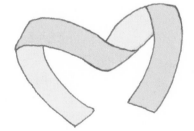

4th

Cut along the line of 2s that runs all the way through the middle. What do you end up with this time?

5th

Take strip number three. Make a half twist in it and tape or glue the ends.

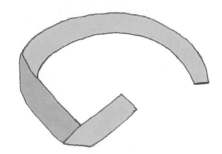

6th

Cut along the line of 3s that are near the edge of the strip. You'll find you're doing a bit more cutting with this one. What do you end up with this time?

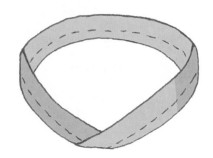

7th

Take strips four and five and loop them together as you would for a paper chain. Then, stick the loops together, slotting one inside the other.

glue here

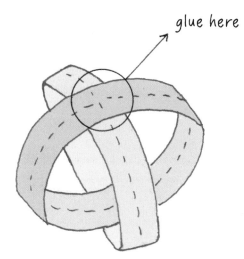

8th

Cut along the center lines of both strips. Can you guess what you'll end up with this time?

I feel like I've been here before!

The möbius strip was discovered by August Möbius, and it is an example of an unusual topological object, because it has only one surface and only one edge.

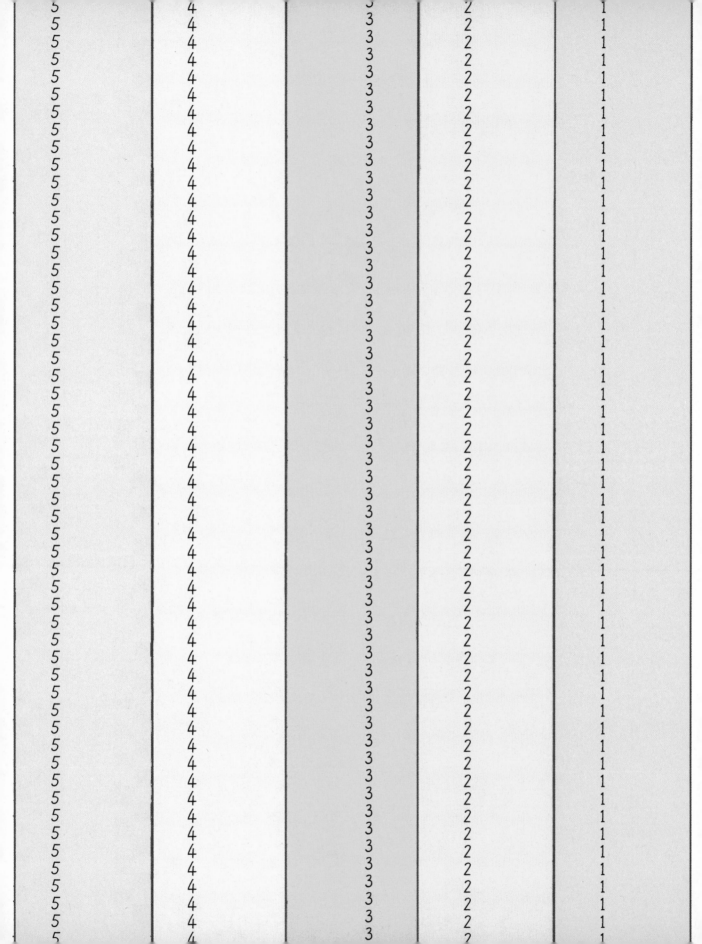

PAPER POLYHEDRA

DO THIS!

Color, cut out, fold and glue these 3D paper shapes,
or "polyhedra." Why not attach a piece of string to
each, and hang them as mathematicool decorations?

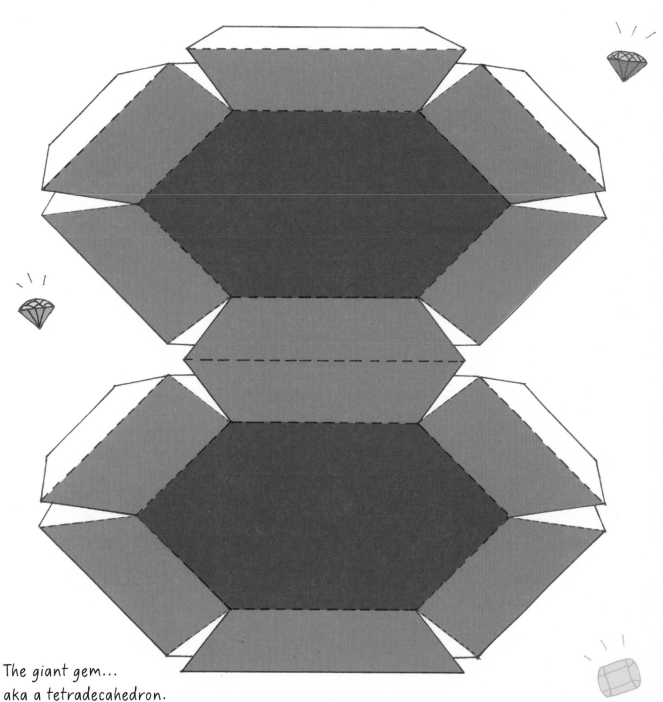

The giant gem...
aka a tetradecahedron.

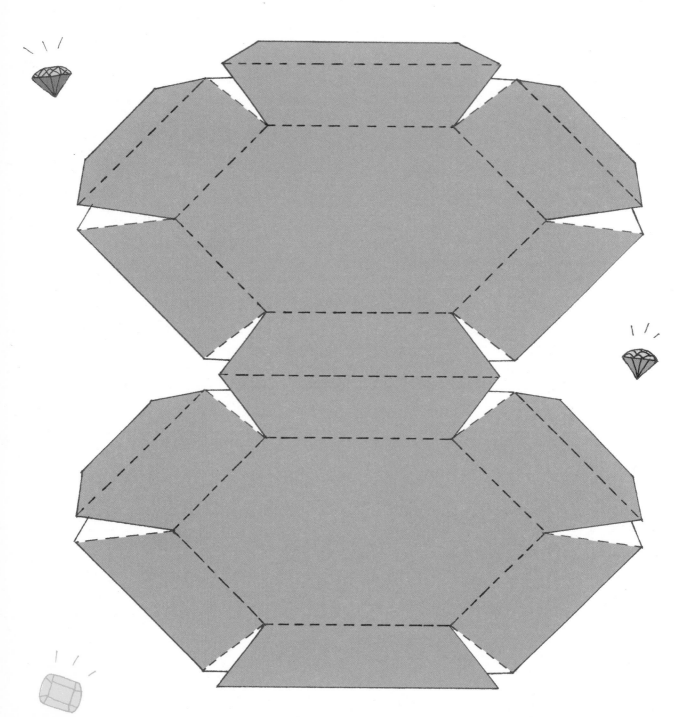

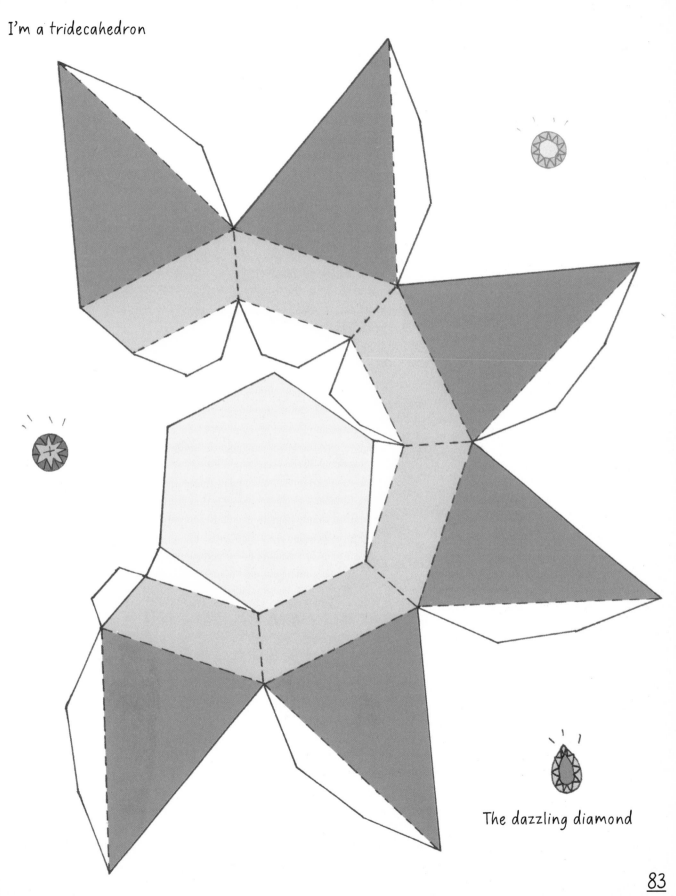

I'm a tridecahedron

The dazzling diamond

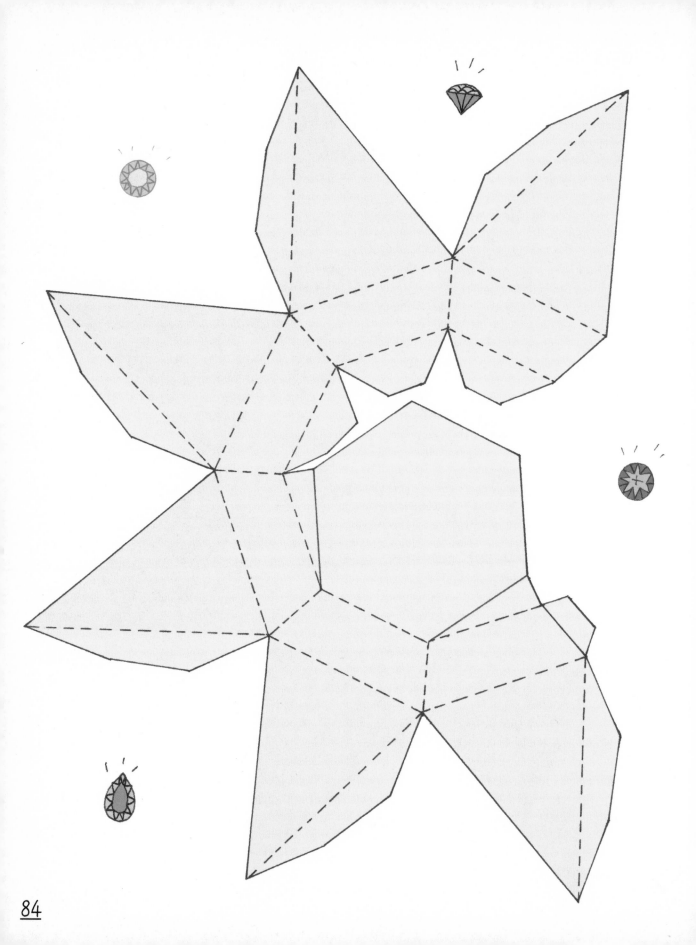

DICE FOR PIG

Cut these dice out, and fold and
glue them into cube shapes.

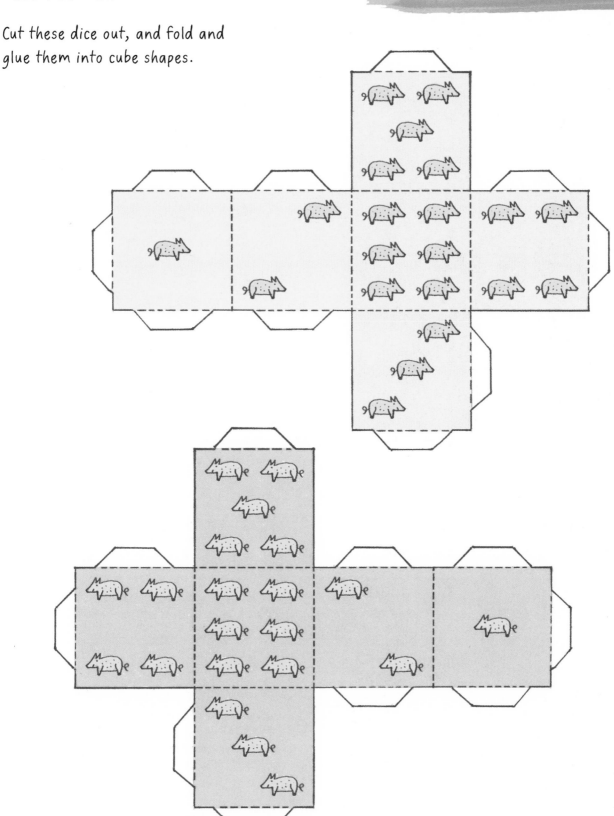

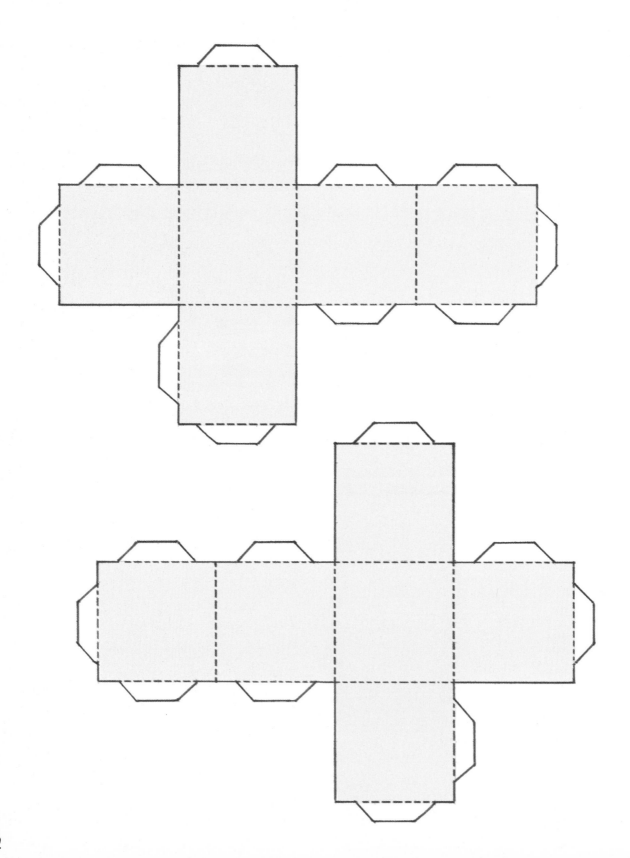

MATH-MAGICAL MIND-READING CARDS

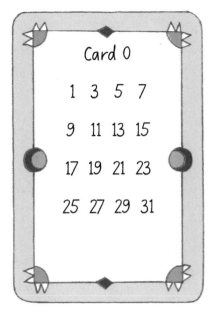

Card 0

1 3 5 7

9 11 13 15

17 19 21 23

25 27 29 31

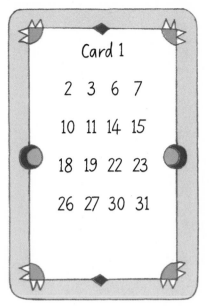

Card 1

2 3 6 7

10 11 14 15

18 19 22 23

26 27 30 31

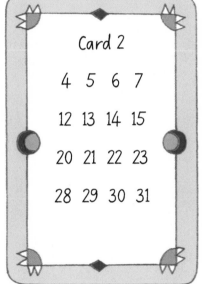

Card 2

4 5 6 7

12 13 14 15

20 21 22 23

28 29 30 31

Card 3

8 9 10 11

12 13 14 15

24 25 26 27

28 29 30 31

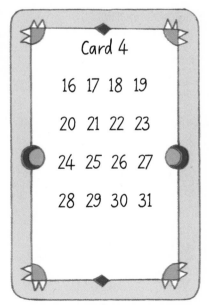

Card 4

16 17 18 19

20 21 22 23

24 25 26 27

28 29 30 31

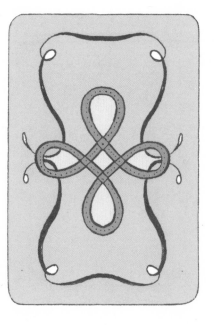

ANSWERS

Pages 8-9

Objects topologically equivalent to a coin include:

a plate, a glass, a cushion, a table, a pencil, an apple, a knife, and many others.

Objects topologically equivalent to a ring include: a drinking straw, a sewing

needle, a wire coat-hanger, or a toilet roll.

Objects topologically similar to a teapot include a pair of leggings, a flip flop,

a plastic shopping bag, or a double-handled casserole pot.

Pages 12-13

The pursuit curves inside a square look like this.

You can color alternate spaces in the design to create a cool effect.

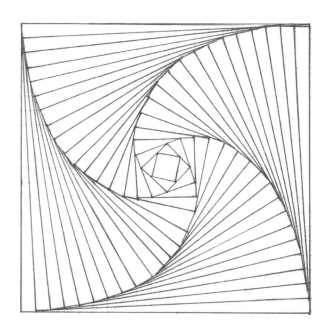 

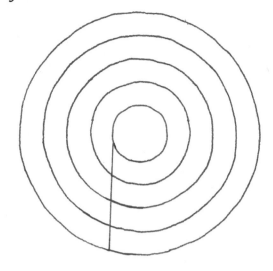

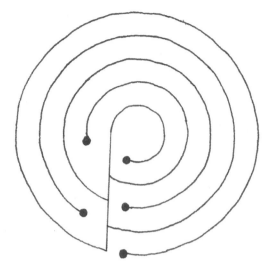

To quickly recreate the simple labyrinth, just draw five concentric circles (circles inside each other), and draw a straight line from the inner circle to the edge.

Next, erase a small part of the circle on alternate sides of the vertical line from the outer circle to the middle.
The labyrinth is complete!

Here the dead ends have all been shaded, revealing the correct path through the maze.

Pages 22-23
It is NOT possible to visit every part of Königsberg without retracing a bridge.
Euler proved that for any graph, you can only trace a line that never crosses itself if
each point on the graph has an even number of lines coming out of it, EXCEPT for the
starting and finishing point which can have an odd number of lines coming out of them.

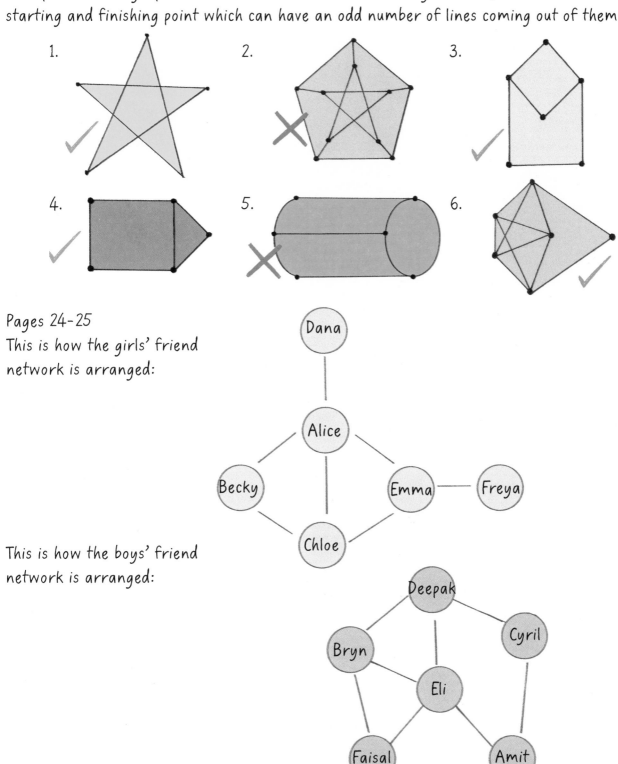

Pages 24-25
This is how the girls' friend
network is arranged:

This is how the boys' friend
network is arranged:

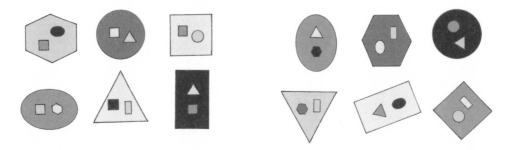

These shapes on the left all have a small square inside them.
The shapes on the right do not contain any small squares.

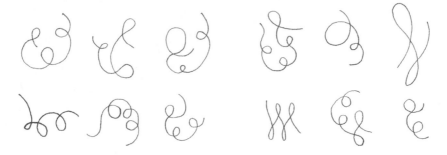

These squiggles on the left all loop over themselves three times.
The squiggles on the right do NOT loop over themselves three times.

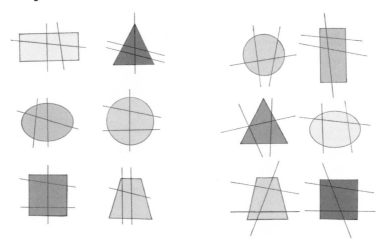

These shapes on the left all have a line running through their middle, along a line of symmetry. The shapes on the right do not have a line down the middle.

If you color the odd and even numbers different colors, you get a "Sierpinski triangle," which is a fractal design similar to the bubble pattern on page 31!

The first diagonal line is just 1s. The second gives you counting numbers, 1, 2, 3, and so on. The third diagonal gives you "triangular numbers."

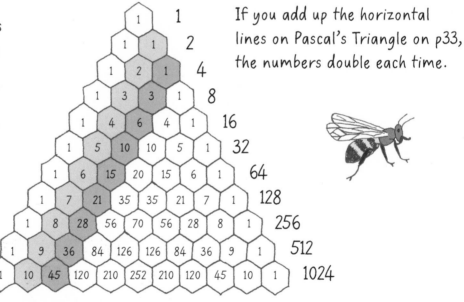

If you add up the horizontal lines on Pascal's Triangle on p33, the numbers double each time.

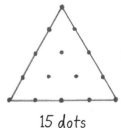

Triangular numbers can be shown by drawing a series of triangles made of dots, and adding a row each time.

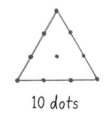

1 dot

3 dots

6 dots

10 dots

15 dots

Pages 34-35
The Caesar Cipher secret message is: "Caesar is a jerk."

Pages 36-37
The encrypted picture

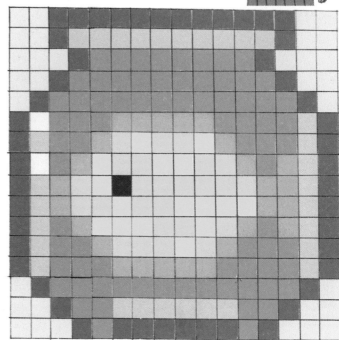

Pages 38-39
The binary picture

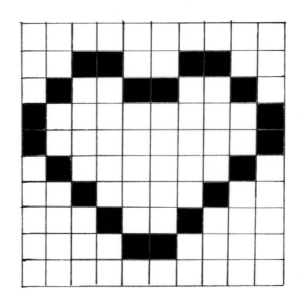

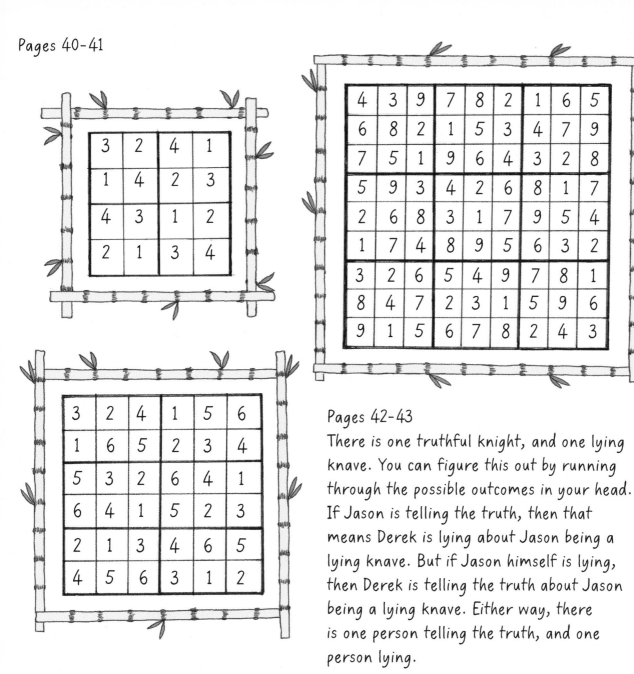

3	2	4	1
1	4	2	3
4	3	1	2
2	1	3	4

4	3	9	7	8	2	1	6	5
6	8	2	1	5	3	4	7	9
7	5	1	9	6	4	3	2	8
5	9	3	4	2	6	8	1	7
2	6	8	3	1	7	9	5	4
1	7	4	8	9	5	6	3	2
3	2	6	5	4	9	7	8	1
8	4	7	2	3	1	5	9	6
9	1	5	6	7	8	2	4	3

3	2	4	1	5	6
1	6	5	2	3	4
5	3	2	6	4	1
6	4	1	5	2	3
2	1	3	4	6	5
4	5	6	3	1	2

Pages 42-43
There is one truthful knight, and one lying knave. You can figure this out by running through the possible outcomes in your head. If Jason is telling the truth, then that means Derek is lying about Jason being a lying knave. But if Jason himself is lying, then Derek is telling the truth about Jason being a lying knave. Either way, there is one person telling the truth, and one person lying.

Pages 63-64
Towers of Hanoi solution: to move the discs from column 1 to column 3 in the smallest number of moves, follow these rules:
- Make the permitted move between column 1 and 2 (in either direction)
- Make the permitted move between column 1 and 3 (in either direction)
- Make the permitted move between column 2 and 3 (in either direction)
- Repeat until complete! This works with any EVEN number of discs, even the mythical 64. However, if you were to try it with 64 discs, moving one disc per second, it would take you around 585 billion years. So no apocalypse just yet.